RODEO
ROUNDUP

WENDY PIRK &
DUANE RADFORD

argenta
press

What is Rodeo?

A rodeo is a contest where cowboys test their ability at events that are based on skills cowboys needed on cattle roundups of the Old West.

Professional rodeos always include bronc riding, bull riding, calf roping, team roping, steer wrestling and barrel racing. Some rodeos have other events, too, like chuckwagon racing, pole bending and mutton busting.

Saddle Bronc

In saddle bronc riding, the rider must stay on the horse's back for 8 seconds as the horse jumps and twists trying to buck him off. He must ride with one hand holding the reins and the other one in the air.

Both the rider and the horse get a score for their performance. The rider gets points for how hard the horse is to ride and how well he controls his body as the horse tries to buck him off.

The horse gets points for how hard it fights to throw the rider off its back. Judges watch for high kicks with straight back legs, spins and twisting.

A horse that bucks sideways gets extra points because it is really hard to ride.

The horse, or bronco, wears a leather strap, called a flank strap, like a belt in front of its back legs. The strap annoys the horse, making it kick higher with its back legs instead of rearing up and lifting its front legs off the ground. It does not hurt the horse and can help keep the rider safer. A rearing horse can crush or fall onto a rider.

Bareback Bronc

Bareback bronc riding has the same rules as saddle bronc, but the rider has no saddle, stirrups or reins to help him stay on the horse. He has only the rigging, a leather handle that looks a lot like a suitcase handle and is attached to a strap that goes around the horse's body, just behind the front legs.

To get a good score, the rider must spur his horse for his entire ride. The spurs must be blunt (no sharp edges) and spin freely so they do not hurt the horse.

Bareback horses are usually smaller and lighter than horses used in saddle bronc riding. They may have less muscle, but they can usually twist and buck faster than saddle bronc horses.

Pickup Rider

During bronc riding events, a pickup rider's job is to help keep the bronc rider safe. If the bronc rider lasts the full 8 seconds on the bronco, the pickup rider rides alongside the bronco so the bronc rider can climb onto the pickup horse's back. The pickup rider also scoops up riders who have fallen off the broncos.

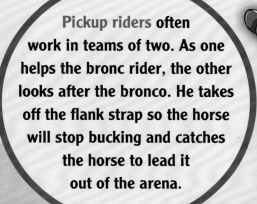

Pickup riders often work in teams of two. As one helps the bronc rider, the other looks after the bronco. He takes off the flank strap so the horse will stop bucking and catches the horse to lead it out of the arena.

In bull riding, the rider has no saddle or reins. He holds onto the end of a rope tied around the bull's body, just behind its front legs. The rider must stay on the bull's back for 8 seconds. He has to hold the rope with one hand and keep his other hand in the air.

Before its turn in the arena, the bull is kept in a small, narrow pen, called a chute. This gives the rider a chance to climb onto the bull's back while the bull is calm. When the rider is ready, the gate to the chute is opened, and the bull bursts into the arena, bucking and twisting.

Bull riding is a lot like bareback bronc riding, only even more dangerous. Bulls weigh more than bareback broncs and are much more aggressive. A bull that throws its rider is more likely to go after the rider than run away.

Bull Riding

Rodeo Clowns

Rodeo clowns might look funny, but their job is one of the most dangerous in a rodeo. Making the crowd laugh between rodeo events so the people don't get bored is the easy part of their job. The hardest and most important part is to distract aggressive bulls that have bucked off their rider.

When a rider is thrown off a bull, he may be hurt or stunned. If he cannot get up right away, he could get kicked, trampled or stabbed by the horns of the angry bull. The rodeo clown keeps the bull busy so the rider can get to safety.

Pickup riders often help distract the bulls, too.

Calf Roping

Calf roping, or tie-down roping, is a timed
event where ropers race, one at a time, to
see who can rope and tie up a calf the fastest.

The horse and rider wait in the box beside the chute that holds the calf. When the calf runs out, it breaks a string tied across the chute. The roper is not allowed to chase the calf until that string breaks. If he leaves the box early, a 10-second penalty is added to his time.

The roper rides after the calf and uses a rope, called a lariat, to lasso the calf around the neck. Once the calf is lassoed, the roper ties the end of the rope to the saddlehorse. The roper jumps off the horse, and the horse pulls back to keep the rope tight.

The roper grabs the calf and throws it onto its side. This move is called flanking.

The roper then ties 3 of the calf's feet together with a special rope, called a piggin' string. Most ropers carry this string in their teeth while they are riding after the calf.

The knot that ties the calf's feet together is called a hooey. Once the roper has finished tying the hooey, he throws his hand into the air, and the time stops.

The roper only gets points if the hooey holds the calf for at least 6 seconds. If the calf can wiggle free earlier, the roper is disqualified.

Some rodeos have an event called breakaway roping, where the calf does not get tied up or thrown to the ground. Instead, when the calf is roped, the rope is tied to the saddle horn with a string. As the calf runs, the rope is pulled tight and the string breaks. The roper's time stops when the string breaks.

Team roping was used in cattle ranching when cowboys needed to catch an animal that was too heavy or strong for one man to deal with on his own.

In this event, two riders work together to rope one steer as quickly as they can. The **header** ropes the steer's head then turns the steer so the **heeler** can rope the steer's back legs. When both riders pull their ropes tight and turn their horses to face each other, the time stops.

Team Roping

Team roping is the only rodeo event that allows men and women to compete together.

The header can use one of three catches to rope the steer. In a clean horn catch, the rope goes around both horns. For a half horn catch, the rope must go around one horn and the neck. If the rope goes around the neck, it is called a neck catch.

All other head catches are not allowed. For example, if the rope goes around the steer's snout or only one horn, it does not count.

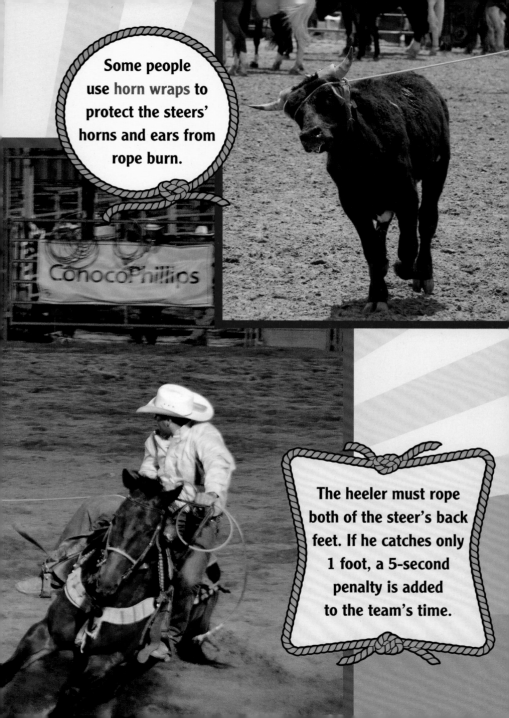

Some people use horn wraps to protect the steers' horns and ears from rope burn.

The heeler must rope both of the steer's back feet. If he catches only 1 foot, a 5-second penalty is added to the team's time.

Steer Wrestling

Steer wrestling, also called bulldogging, is one of rodeo's quickest events. The world record for steer wrestling is less than 2.5 seconds, though runs usually last closer to 7 seconds.

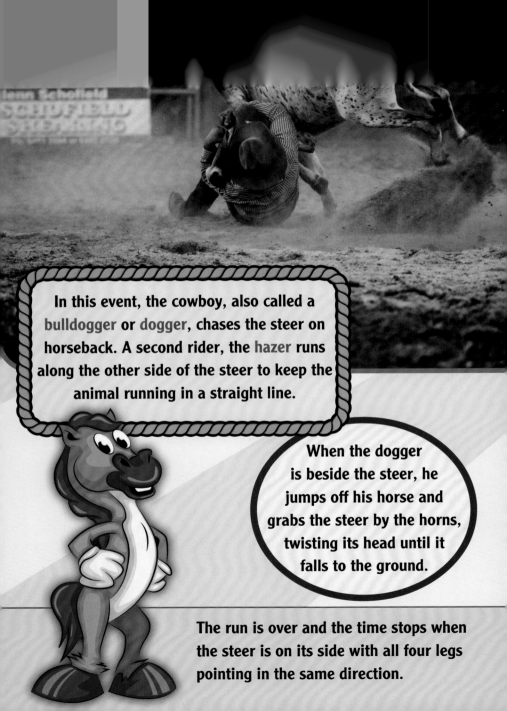

In this event, the cowboy, also called a bulldogger or dogger, chases the steer on horseback. A second rider, the hazer runs along the other side of the steer to keep the animal running in a straight line.

When the dogger is beside the steer, he jumps off his horse and grabs the steer by the horns, twisting its head until it falls to the ground.

The run is over and the time stops when the steer is on its side with all four legs pointing in the same direction.

The Chuckwagon Race

Each group in a chuckwagon race is made up of the driver, his team of 4 horses and the outriders. There used to be 4 outriders per chuckwagon, but now there are only 2.

When the bell or horn sounds, the outriders have to load a camp stove into the back of the chuckwagon. In some rodeos, they also have to load tent poles.

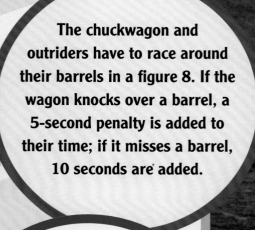

The chuckwagon and outriders have to race around their barrels in a figure 8. If the wagon knocks over a barrel, a 5-second penalty is added to their time; if it misses a barrel, 10 seconds are added.

When they are finished going around the barrels, the chuckwagon and outriders race once around the racetrack. The outriders have to finish the race after the chuckwagon, but if they are too far behind they get a penalty.

The first time a chuckwagon race was held during a rodeo was at the Calgary Stampede in 1923.

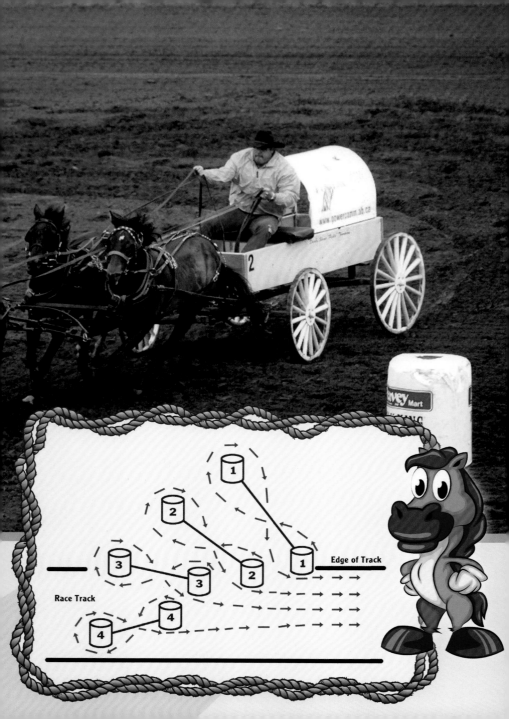

Edge of Track

Race Track

Barrel Racing

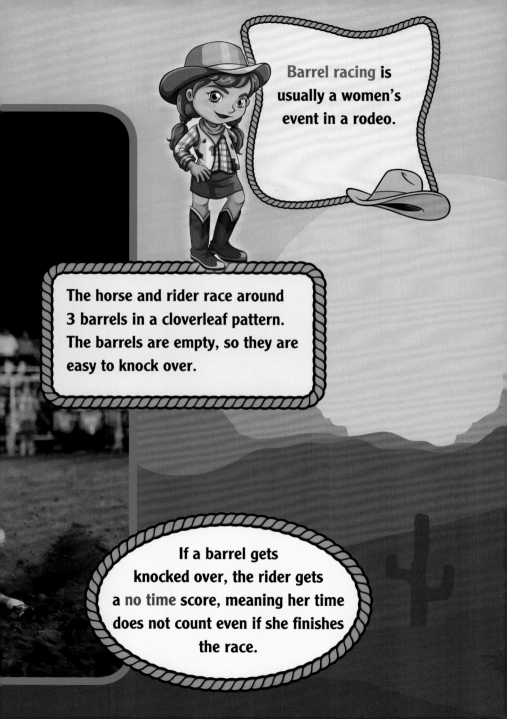

Barrel racing is usually a women's event in a rodeo.

The horse and rider race around 3 barrels in a cloverleaf pattern. The barrels are empty, so they are easy to knock over.

If a barrel gets knocked over, the rider gets a no time score, meaning her time does not count even if she finishes the race.

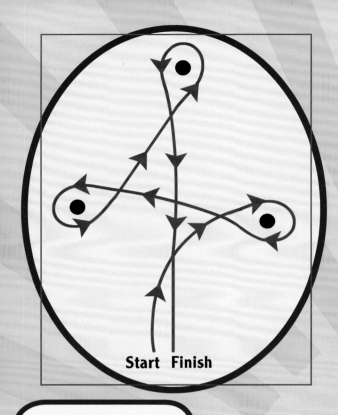

Start Finish

This is the cloverleaf pattern a horse and rider must follow if they choose to run the course with a right start. The rider can also choose to start the course heading left after crossing the starting line.

A rider will get a no time score if her horse makes a mistake running the cloverleaf pattern, or she falls off the horse during the race.

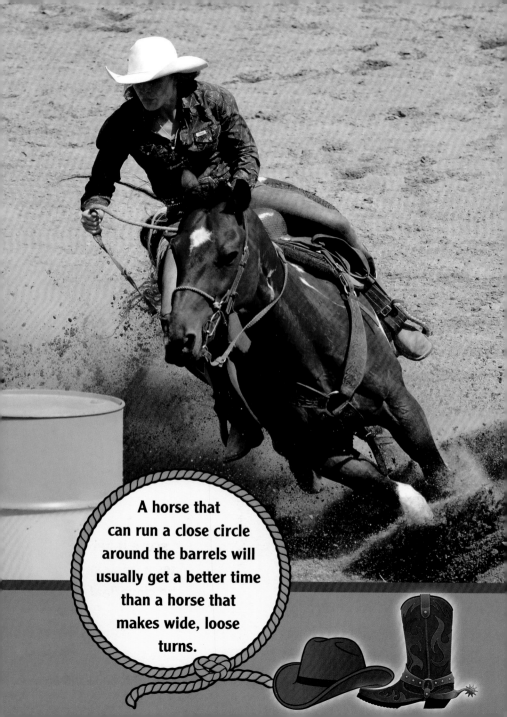

A horse that can run a close circle around the barrels will usually get a better time than a horse that makes wide, loose turns.

In **pole bending**, the rider races her horse in a zig-zag pattern in and out of 6 poles.

The horse and rider must run the course as quickly as possible without knocking down any poles. They don't get a penalty if they touch a pole, but there is a 5-second penalty for each pole that falls over.

This is the pattern the horse must follow through the poles. If the horse makes a mistake in the pattern, the rider is disqualified.

Finish · Start

In this event, the horse gets a running start. The time starts when the horse's nose crosses the starting line. This helps the horse run the race faster than if it had to start from a standstill.

Pole Bending

Trick Riding

Trick riding first began as a contest in Wild West shows. It was once a competition in rodeos, too. Riders were judged on their costumes, how hard their tricks were and how well the horse performed.

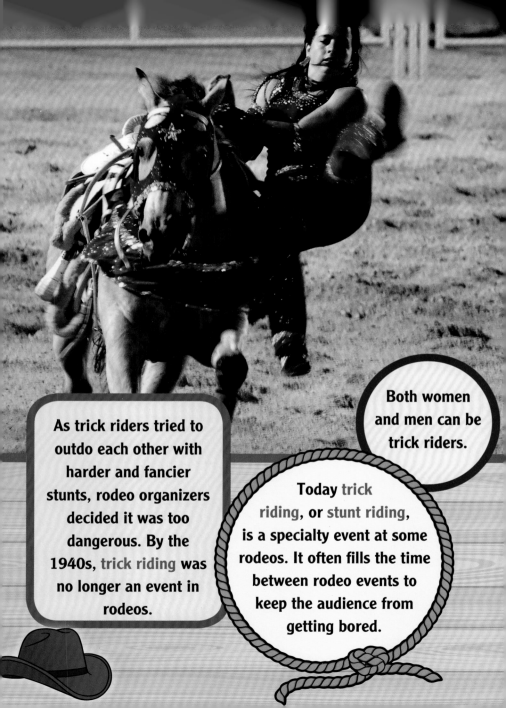

As trick riders tried to outdo each other with harder and fancier stunts, rodeo organizers decided it was too dangerous. By the 1940s, trick riding was no longer an event in rodeos.

Both women and men can be trick riders.

Today trick riding, or stunt riding, is a specialty event at some rodeos. It often fills the time between rodeo events to keep the audience from getting bored.

These are some of the classic tricks:

The **Death Drag** or **Cossack Drag**

The **Apache Hideaway** or **Backward Fender**

Roman Riding

The Spritz Stand

The Hippodrome

Mutton Busting

In this event, kids between 4 and 7 years old try to ride a sheep as it runs around the arena.

Some kids make it look easy.

Some not so much.

The kids must weigh less than 60 pounds (27 kilograms) so they do not hurt the sheep's back. They have no saddle or reins to hold on to, only wool.

Different rodeos have different rules for mutton busting. Some say the kids have to ride the sheep for 6 seconds. Others say whoever rides the longest wins.

Rodeo History

The first rodeos were just small gatherings of cowboys showing off the skills they needed to do their jobs herding cattle. The cowboys may have placed small bets on who was the best roper or who could stay on a bronc the longest.

In the past, some cowboys made their living by broncbusting. Broncs or broncos were wild horses that needed to be "broken" or tamed so that they would wear a saddle and carry a rider. This is where today's saddle bronc event comes from.

Roping was another important skill a cowboy needed to do his job well. During cattle drives, cowboys might have to rope a runaway cow or calf to keep it with the herd. Sick or wounded animals would also be roped so they could be given medicine or have their injuries taken care of.

During the yearly roundup, when cowboys went out to collect their cattle from the open range, calves were roped so they could be branded.

Roping is the only rodeo skill that is still used on cattle ranches today.

Bull riding and steer wrestling were never part of a cowboy's job. These events probably came about as cowboys looked for new ways to prove they were stronger and braver than their fellow cowboys.

Wild West Show

BUFFALO BILL'S WILD WEST
AND CONGRESS OF ROUGH RIDERS OF THE WORLD.

COL. W. F. CODY
BUFFALO BILL
WILL APPEAR
AT EVERY PERFORMANCE

A COMPANY OF WILD WEST COWBOYS. THE REAL ROUGH RIDERS OF THE WORLD WHOSE DARING EXPLOITS HAVE MADE THEIR VERY NAMES SYNONYMOUS WITH DEEDS OF BRAVERY.

Modern day rodeos grew out of the Wild West Shows that were popular in the U.S. during the late 1800s and early 1900s.

The most famous Wild West Show of all time was Buffalo Bill's Wild West show. His show was based on "roping, riding and shooting," where cowboys wowed the crowd with their skills. It was part rodeo and part theater, and he put on "cowboy and Indian shows" where both groups acted out battles and other scenes like train robberies.

Many famous people starred in Buffalo Bill's show, including Annie Oakley, a well-known sharpshooter, and Chief Sitting Bull, a Lakota holy man known for his role in the Battle of Little Big Horn.

Calgary Stampede

Guy Weadick was an American performer who wanted to create a show as huge as Buffalo Bill's but without the theater. He wanted his show to be a competition for cowboys to show off their roping and riding skills. In 1912 he organized the first Calgary Stampede.

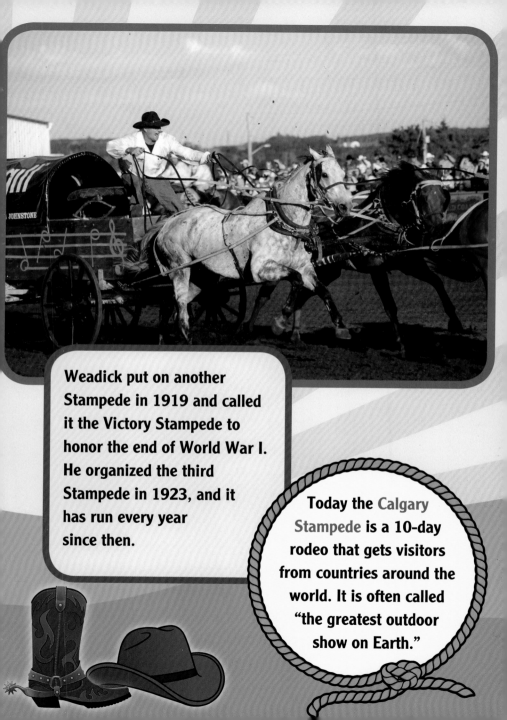

Weadick put on another Stampede in 1919 and called it the Victory Stampede to honor the end of World War I. He organized the third Stampede in 1923, and it has run every year since then.

Today the Calgary Stampede is a 10-day rodeo that gets visitors from countries around the world. It is often called "the greatest outdoor show on Earth."

Other events at the Stampede include a parade, a midway and pancake breakfasts. There is also a grandstand show every night that ends with fireworks.

The Stampede is famous for its free pancake breakfasts. The tradition started in 1923 when Jack Morton, a chuckwagon driver, invited anyone who walked by his tent to join him for breakfast. Today free pancake breakfasts are held all over Calgary every day of the Stampede.

The midway is also famous, and not only for its rides. Every year food trucks on the midway dream up crazy foods to serve during the Stampede. Hot dog-stuffed pickles, deep-fried butter tarts, deep-fried coffee and doughnut burgers are only a few of the weird foods that have been served.

Canadian Finals Rodeo

cfr.ca

RODEO

The Canadian Finals Rodeo (CFR) is a 5-day event held in Edmonton, Alberta, every November. It is the last competition of the year for the Canadian Professional Rodeo Association.

Only the top 10 point scorers of the year from Pro Rodeo Canada and the cowboys who earn first and second place in the last 10 rodeos in the Canadian Rodeo Tour can compete in the CFR.

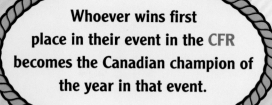

Whoever wins first place in their event in the CFR becomes the Canadian champion of the year in that event.

The CFR used to be open only to Canadian cowboys, but now cowboys from any country can compete as long as they qualify.

National Finals Rodeo

The National Finals Rodeo (NFR) is a 10-day event held every December in Las Vegas, Nevada. It is the top championship rodeo event in the U.S.

The **NFR** is often called the "Super Bowl of Rodeo."

Cowboys who compete in the **NFR** are battling to become the world champion in their event. **NFR** events include saddle bronc riding, bareback bronc riding, bull riding, calf roping, team roping, steer wrestling and barrel racing.

Rodeo Essentials

A cowboy isn't a cowboy without his hat. The wide brim helps keep the sun out of the cowboy's eyes, and it helps keep him dry when it rains. In some rodeo events, though, like bull riding, the cowboy has to wear a helmet instead of his hat to protect his head in case he falls off of the bucking animal.

Made of leather, chaps strap on over the cowboy's legs. Chaps protect working cowboys' legs from burs and sharp brush as they ride their horses. In a rodeo, chaps protect the legs from cuts and scrapes if a rider gets thrown off his horse or bull.

A good pair of gloves helps a cowboy hold onto the reins or rope. Gloves also protect the hands from rope burn. Some bronc and bull riders put a dab of glue or some 2-sided tape on their gloves (and sometimes boots) to help them keep their grip.

Back in the old cowboy days, the most important thing a cowboy owned was his saddle. A properly fitted saddle can bring out the best in your horse.

Many cowboys competing in bull or bronc riding events wear a padded vest to protect them in case they get kicked or thrown off the animal.

Cowboy boots were designed with the working cowboy in mind. They go high on the leg to protect it from getting scraped by brush while the cowboy is riding his horse. They have high heels so they will not slip out of the stirrup. The toe of the boot is narrow so it can fit easily into the stirrup.

Some saddle bronc riders wear boots that are a bit too big when they ride. That way if one of their feet gets caught in a stirrup when they are bucked off, their foot will slide out of the boot and they won't be dragged on the ground behind the horse.

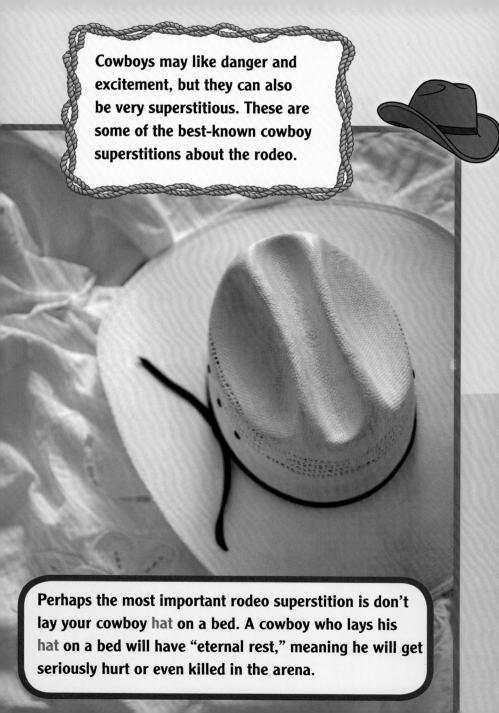

Cowboys may like danger and excitement, but they can also be very superstitious. These are some of the best-known cowboy superstitions about the rodeo.

Perhaps the most important rodeo superstition is don't lay your cowboy hat on a bed. A cowboy who lays his hat on a bed will have "eternal rest," meaning he will get seriously hurt or even killed in the arena.

Don't ride with change in your pocket, or that's all the money you will ever earn in a rodeo (meaning the cowboy will always lose his event).

Rodeo Superstitions

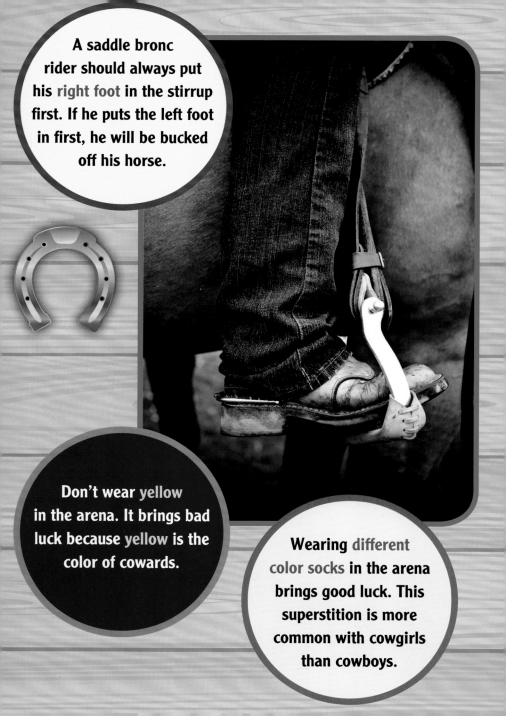

A saddle bronc rider should always put his right foot in the stirrup first. If he puts the left foot in first, he will be bucked off his horse.

Don't wear yellow in the arena. It brings bad luck because yellow is the color of cowards.

Wearing different color socks in the arena brings good luck. This superstition is more common with cowgirls than cowboys.

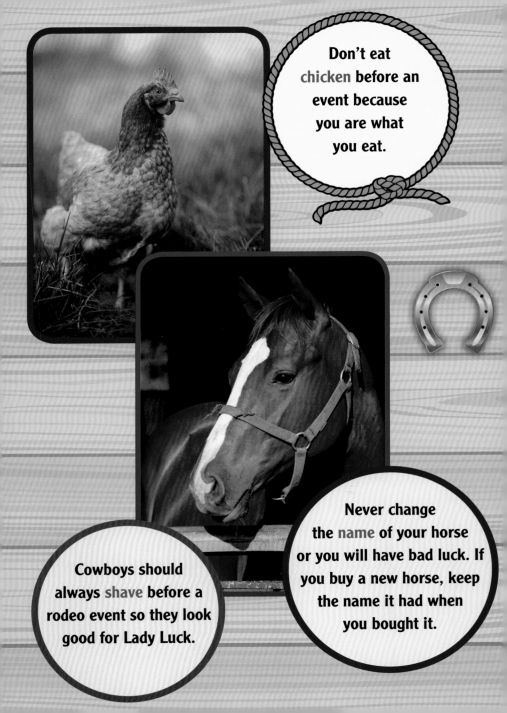

Don't eat chicken before an event because you are what you eat.

Never change the name of your horse or you will have bad luck. If you buy a new horse, keep the name it had when you bought it.

Cowboys should always shave before a rodeo event so they look good for Lady Luck.

First printed in 2016 10 9 8 7 6 5 4 3 2 1

Printed in China

The Publisher: Argenta Press is an imprint of Dragon Hill Publishing Ltd.

Library and Archives Canada Cataloguing in Publication

Pirk, Wendy, 1973-, author Rodeo roundup / Wendy Pirk and Duane Radford.

Issued in print and electronic formats.

ISBN 978-1-896124-63-6 (softcover)
ISBN 978-1-896124-64-3 (EPUB)

1. Rodeos—Juvenile literature. 2. Rodeos—History—Juvenile literature. 3. Cowboys—Juvenile literature. I. Radford, Duane, 1946–, author II. Title.

GV1834.P57 2017   j791.8'4   C2017-902225-3
                                                   C2017-902226-1

Front cover credits: leaf/Thinkstock; gribben/Thinkstock; dgphotography/Thinkstock; dobric/Thinkstock; macrovector/ Thinkstock

Back cover credits: Jupiterimages/Thinkstock; Allevinatis/Thinkstock; lukpedclub/Thinkstock; dgphotography/Thinkstock; macrovector/Thinkstock

Photo credits: Duane Radford, 24, 28–29, 49. From Flickr: a4gpa, 8, 12a, 16; alh1, 38b, 39c; Calgary reviews, 17, 48; Emilio, 12b; IQRemix, 52, 53; Larry Lamsa, 4, 5, 7, 22–23, 32–33, 36, 37, 38a, 40a&b, 41a&b; Jasonwoodhead23, 51b; Jeremy Howard, 58b; Ken Bosma, 20–21; Petra Koenig, 51a; ralph arvesen, 30–31; Tony Sergo, 2, 6, 10, 11, 13, 14b, 15a&b, 25, 56b; William Bigelis, 3; xlibber, 26-27. From Library of Congress, 39a, 42a&b, 43a&b, 44b, 47. From Thinkstock: acceptfoto, 63; alptraum, 19; arinahabich, 59; dgphotography, 14a, 34; Edoma, 39b; gribben, 35; Jacek_Sopotnicki, 57; Janessanother-dayinmylife, 9; Jupiterimages, 62; killashandra, 18; KonstantinPetkov, 63a; Plez, 23a; Purestock, 58a; redrex, 61; rja, 50a; RobertCrum, 57; sfmorris, 56; St.Marie.Ltd, 44a; Thinkstock, 60. From Wikipedia: Cpl Matt Millham, 54–55.

All diagrams were adapted by Tamara Hartson based on: image from World Professional Chuckwagon Association, 29; image by Katie Ockert, 32; image from Wikipedia, 53.

Cowboy Icons, Ropes and Characters: blueringmedia/Thinkstock, Glam-Y/Thinkstock, larryrains/Thinkstock, lawangdesign/ Thinkstock, Moriz89/Thinkstock, seamartini/Thinkstock, skalapendra/Thinkstock, Vectalex/Thinkstock.

Background Graphics: mushroomstore/Thinkstock, 2–3, 10–11, 26–26, 30–31, 46–47, 54–55; yukipon/Thinkstock, 37, 38–39, 42–43, 44–45, 58–59, 62–63.

Produced with the assistance of the Government of Alberta, Alberta Media Fund.

We acknowledge the financial support of the Government of Canada.

Funded by the Government of Canada
Financé par le gouvernement du Canada | Canadä

PC: 28